The Emerald Tablet of Thoth

Ancient Alchemical Wisdom for Spiritual Transformation

A Modern Translation

Adapted for the Contemporary Reader

Attributed to Thoth Hermes Trismegistus

Table of Contents

Preface - Message to the Reader

Rebuilding the Greatest Library in Human History

Thousands of years ago, the Library of Alexandria was the heart of global knowledge — a sanctuary where the wisdom of every known civilization was gathered and shared freely.

And then, it was lost.

Now, we're rebuilding it — and you are invited to join us.

At the Library of Alexandria, we've set out to make every book available to *every person on Earth* — not just in print, but in every language, every format, and for every reader.

Here's how we do it:

- **Deluxe Print Editions at True Printing Cost** - Order any book as a high-quality paperback, elegant hardcover, or stunning boxset — and only pay what it costs to print. No markups. No middlemen.
- **Unlimited Access to the Greatest Works** - Enjoy thousands of timeless classics — from Plato to Shakespeare to Tolstoy — in beautiful, modern eBook and audiobook editions. Read and listen without limits — for every reader, everywhere.
- **Modern Translations for Every Language & Dialect** - We're reimagining the classics in clear, accessible language — and translating them into every dialect imaginable. Everyone deserves to understand humanity's greatest ideas.

When you visit **LibraryofAlexandria.com**, you're not just accessing books — you're joining a global movement to restore, preserve, and share the wisdom of civilization.

Join us today at LibraryofAlexandria.com

Together, we'll ensure the light of human wisdom never fades again.

With gratitude,
The Modern Library of Alexandria Team

Visit:

www.libraryofalexandria.com

Or scan the code below:

Introduction

The Origins of an Enigmatic Text: Thoth, Hermes Trismegistus, and the Alchemical Tradition

Few texts in the history of esoteric thought have generated as much fascination, mystique, and interpretive depth as The Emerald Tablet, attributed to the legendary Thoth Hermes Trismegistus. This short, cryptic document—comprising only a few lines—has served as a cornerstone for alchemical philosophy, Hermetic mysticism, and spiritual transformation across centuries and cultures. Revered by alchemists, magicians, mystics, and metaphysicians alike, The Emerald Tablet speaks in a voice at once ancient and eternal, articulating a vision of cosmic unity, divine correspondence, and the soul's potential for transmutation.

Attributed to Thoth, the Egyptian god of wisdom, writing, and magic—who was later merged with the Greek Hermes to become Hermes Trismegistus ("the thrice-greatest")—the Tablet is said to reveal the secret of the prima materia: the source and essence of all things. It proclaims a universal axiom of Hermeticism: "As above, so below." In this simple yet profound phrase lies the key to a vision of reality in which the microcosm reflects the macrocosm, and the spiritual journey mirrors the processes of nature. To understand this principle is to unlock the door to alchemical transmutation—not merely the transformation of base metals into gold, but of the human soul into its divine form.

While its origins remain shrouded in mystery, The Emerald Tablet likely first appeared in Arabic sources between the 6th and 8th centuries and was translated into Latin in the 12th century by scholars like Hugo of Santalla. It quickly became central to the Western alchemical tradition, influencing figures such as Albertus Magnus, Roger Bacon, Paracelsus, and Isaac Newton, who composed his own translation and commentary on the text. The Tablet became not only a symbol of hidden wisdom but a practical guide to spiritual realization and metaphysical insight.

This modern edition, Ancient Alchemical Wisdom for Spiritual Transformation – A Modern Translation – Adapted for the Contemporary Reader, seeks to preserve the mystical potency of the original while rendering its insights accessible and relevant for today's spiritual seekers. In doing so, it honors the legacy of

Hermeticism as both a spiritual science and a sacred art—a discipline of inner refinement and divine remembrance.

"As Above, So Below":
The Doctrine of Correspondence and the Alchemical Cosmos

The most famous line of The Emerald Tablet—"As above, so below; as below, so above"—summarizes the Hermetic worldview in its most distilled form. This doctrine of correspondence posits that the structure of the cosmos is mirrored in all things, from the movements of stars to the inner workings of the human soul. There is no strict division between matter and spirit, heaven and earth, divine and mortal. Rather, all levels of reality participate in a unified order, governed by universal principles and animated by a single divine intelligence.

In alchemical terms, this correspondence enables transformation. Just as metals can be refined through fire, the soul can be purified through discipline, contemplation, and inner work. The Tablet speaks of the "One Thing," a mysterious substance that underlies all existence, and whose operations produce both the material world and spiritual awakening. To discover this

"One Thing" within oneself is to realize the true work of alchemy: not the accumulation of power or wealth, but the alignment with cosmic truth.

The language of the Tablet is deliberately paradoxical. It describes the process by which "the subtle triumphs over the gross," how the sun is its father and the moon its mother, and how it rises from earth to heaven and then returns again. These alchemical metaphors conceal multiple layers of meaning: physical, psychological, spiritual, and cosmological. They invite the reader not merely to decode them, but to meditate on them, allowing their symbols to awaken insight through contemplation.

From a modern perspective, these teachings echo discoveries in systems theory, depth psychology, and spiritual ecology. The idea that all things are interconnected, that consciousness shapes reality, and that transformation arises from the balance of opposites, finds resonance in both ancient Hermetic thought and contemporary science. Thus, The Emerald Tablet endures not as an obsolete relic, but as a vibrant articulation of perennial wisdom.

Why The Emerald Tablet Belongs in the Modern Canon of Sacred Philosophy

Despite its brevity, The Emerald Tablet has exerted an influence disproportionate to its length. It encapsulates an entire cosmology, a system of ethics, and a spiritual path in just a few lines. In doing so, it functions like a seed—small, but capable of unfolding into a vast tree of understanding. Its presence in the Complete Socratic, Platonic, and Mystical Traditions is not only justified, but vital, for it provides a bridge between ancient Egyptian theology, Greek philosophy, and the later Western esoteric tradition.

What sets the Tablet apart is its universality. It speaks in a language that transcends dogma, nationality, and religious denomination. Its truths are not bound to any one faith or metaphysical system, but are expressed in archetypal symbols that resonate across cultures. Its call is to inner transformation, divine remembrance, and the reintegration of human consciousness with the cosmos.

The Tablet's inclusion in this modern edition acknowledges the need for spiritual texts that do not merely instruct but initiate. The reading of The Emerald Tablet is not passive; it is an act of participation in a lineage of seekers who have looked beyond surface appearances into the deeper patterns of existence. Whether read as a cryptic poem, an alchemical manual, or a meditative oracle, the Tablet invites the reader into a process of becoming: of refining the self into its most luminous form.

In an age overwhelmed by materialism, fragmentation, and disconnection, The Emerald Tablet offers a radiant counterpoint. It reminds us that within the chaos of the world lies an order, and within the heart of the individual lies a spark of divine intelligence. To read it today is to take a step on the same path that sages, scientists, mystics, and magicians have walked for centuries: the path of integration, illumination, and transformation.

As you begin this modern translation, allow its words to work on multiple levels. Do not rush to interpret. Read slowly, reflect deeply, and let the ancient wisdom of Thoth—Hermes Trismegistus—stir within you the memory of the One Thing that is the source of all. For in that remembrance lies the true meaning of alchemy, and the purpose of the spiritual life itself.

The Emerald Tablets Of
Thoth the Atlantean

The story behind these tablets is unusual and may seem unbelievable to modern scientists. They are said to be incredibly ancient, going back around 36,000 years before the common era. The author is Thoth, an Atlantean priest-king, who established a colony in Egypt after the destruction of Atlantis.

Thoth is credited with building the Great Pyramid of Giza, though it has been wrongly attributed to Cheops. In the pyramid, he stored his knowledge and preserved the records and tools from ancient Atlantis. Thoth ruled over Egypt for about 16,000 years, from around 52,000 to 36,000 BCE. Under his leadership, the once primitive people of Egypt rose to a high level of civilization.

Thoth had overcome death and could pass from life only when he chose, without actually dying. His great wisdom made him ruler over many Atlantean colonies, including those in South and Central America. When it was time for him to leave Egypt, he built the Great Pyramid over the entrance to the Halls of Amenti, where he placed his records and selected the most worthy people to guard his secrets.

In later times, these guardians became the priests of the pyramids, and Thoth was worshiped as a god of wisdom and the Recorder. In the age that followed his departure, the Halls of Amenti became known in legend as the underworld, where souls went after death for judgment.

Thoth's spirit continued to incarnate in human form, as described in the tablets. He returned three times, with his last appearance as Hermes, known as the "thrice-born." During this incarnation, he left behind writings known as the Emerald Tablets, a later and more simplified version of the ancient mysteries.

The tablets translated in this work are ten in total, originally placed in the Great Pyramid under the care of the pyramid priests. For convenience, the content has been divided into thirteen sections. The final two tablets contain such powerful knowledge that it is currently forbidden to release them to the public. However, the ones included here hold valuable secrets for those who are serious about seeking wisdom. They should not be read just once but studied many times, as only through careful reading can their deeper meanings be understood. A casual reading will provide glimpses of beauty, but true insight comes only through deep study.

Now, let me explain how these ancient secrets were brought back to light after being hidden for so long. Around 1,300 BCE, Egypt was in turmoil, and many priests were sent to other parts of the world. Among them were some of the pyramid priests carrying the Emerald Tablets. They used the tablets as a symbol of authority, allowing them to influence less advanced priesthoods in other regions descended from Atlantean colonies.

These priests eventually settled in South America, where they found the Mayan civilization, which had preserved much of the ancient wisdom. The priests stayed with the Mayans, and by the 10th century, the Mayan people had established themselves in the Yucatan. The Emerald Tablets were placed under the altar of a great Sun Temple.

After the Spanish conquest, the Mayan cities were abandoned, and the treasures within their temples were forgotten. It's important to understand that the Great Pyramid has always been a temple for initiation into the mysteries. Even figures like Jesus, Solomon, and Apollonius were initiated there.

The author of this translation, who is connected to the Great White Lodge that works through the pyramid priesthood, was instructed to retrieve the tablets and return them to the Great Pyramid. After many adventures, the tablets were recovered. Before returning them, permission was granted to translate and keep a copy of the wisdom they contain. This translation was completed in 1925, and only now has permission been given to release part of it to the public. Some people will doubt its authenticity, but true seekers will find wisdom within these words. If the light is already within you, the light in these tablets will resonate with your soul.

Now, let me describe the physical nature of the tablets. They are made of a bright emerald-green material, created through a process of alchemical transformation. These tablets are imperishable and immune to all natural elements, with their atomic structure remaining stable forever. In this way, they defy the natural laws of matter and ionization.

The ancient Atlantean language is engraved on their surfaces, and these inscriptions respond to focused thoughts, releasing mental vibrations that awaken understanding in the reader. The tablets are held together by hoops of a golden-colored alloy, suspended from a rod made of the same material.

The knowledge within these tablets forms the foundation of the ancient mysteries. Anyone who reads them with an open mind will greatly expand their wisdom. Read them, believe or not, but read them—and the vibrations within will awaken a response in your soul.

In the following pages, I will reveal some of the deeper mysteries hinted at in previous writings. Humanity's search for the laws that govern life has been constant, but the truth has always been hidden just beyond the veil that separates the higher realms from the material world. Those who seek knowledge must learn to look inward, for the answers lie in silence, beyond the distractions of the physical senses. Those who talk do not know, and those who know do not speak.

The highest truths cannot be spoken, for they exist beyond words and symbols. Symbols serve as keys to understanding deeper truths, but often people cannot see what lies beyond the symbols because they seem too overwhelming. If we realize that all material symbols are just representations of higher truths, we begin to develop the vision to see beyond the veil.

Everything in the universe moves according to law. The laws that govern the planets are no different from the laws that shape human life. One of the most important Cosmic Laws is the one that connects the material aspect of humanity with the spiritual. The key to this connection lies in the intellectual part of human nature, which bridges the material and spiritual worlds.

Those who seek higher knowledge must strengthen their minds and concentrate all their energy on their chosen path. The search for light, life, and love begins on the material plane, but it reaches its ultimate goal in complete unity with the universal consciousness. The material world is only the starting point; the true goal is spiritual enlightenment.

In the following pages, I will interpret the Emerald Tablets and reveal some of their hidden meanings. The words of Thoth contain many layers of truth, and these hidden meanings will become clear with thoughtful reflection. If your own inner light is awakened, the knowledge within these tablets will resonate with your soul.

TABLET 1 I, Thoth, the Atlantean, master of ancient mysteries, keeper of sacred knowledge, and mighty ruler, have lived through countless generations. As I prepare to enter the Halls of Amenti, I write down this wisdom for those who come after me. In the great city of Keor, on the island of Undal, I began this life long ago. The people of Atlantis were not like the men of today—they did not live short lives, but instead, they renewed their existence over and over through the Halls of Amenti, where the river of life flows eternally.

I have traveled down the dark path that leads to light a hundred times over, and just as many times I have returned from darkness, renewed in strength and power. Now, I leave once more, and the people of Khem (ancient Egypt) will no longer see me. But one day, I will rise again, mighty and powerful, to demand an account from those I left behind. Beware, people of Khem, if you have betrayed my teachings, for I will cast you down into the darkness from which you came.

Do not reveal my secrets to those from the North or the South, or my curse will fall upon you. Remember my words, for I will return and demand from you all that you have been entrusted with. Even from beyond time and death, I will return to reward or punish you according to how you have followed my truths.

My people were great in ancient times, far greater than the people who live now. We held knowledge that reached into the depths of the universe, uncovering wisdom from Earth's earliest days. We were wise with the knowledge of the Children of Light, who lived among us, and we drew power from the eternal fire.

Among us, the greatest of all men was my father, Thotme, the keeper of the great temple and the link between the Children of Light and the people who lived across the ten islands of Atlantis. He was the voice of the Dweller of Unal, whose words the kings obeyed.

I grew up under my father's guidance, learning the ancient mysteries, and the fire of wisdom grew within me until it consumed my soul. On a great day, the Dweller of the Temple summoned me before him. Few men had looked upon his face and lived, for the Children of Light, when not in physical form, are not like the sons of men. I was chosen from among humanity to be taught by the Dweller, so that I might carry out his purposes, which were not yet born in the world.

For long ages, I lived in the temple, learning ever more wisdom until I reached the light of the great fire. The Dweller taught me the path to Amenti, the underworld where the great king sits on his throne of power. I bowed before the Lords of Life and Death, and they gave me the Key of Life. I was freed from the cycle of death and rebirth. I traveled to the stars, where space and time meant nothing, and after drinking deeply from the cup of wisdom, I looked into the hearts of men. There, I discovered even greater mysteries, and my soul was at peace.

Throughout the ages, I have watched people die and be reborn in the light of life. But as Atlantis declined, the consciousness that had once been one with me faded, replaced by lesser beings from distant stars. Following the laws of the universe, the word of the Master began to take form. The thoughts of the Atlanteans turned downward into darkness, and the Dweller awoke from his detachment, calling forth his power. Deep in the heart of the Earth, the Sons of Amenti heard his call. Using the power of the Logos, they directed the eternal fire, shifting its course.

A great flood swept over the world, shifting the balance of the Earth, and only the Temple of Light remained standing on the mountain of Undal, still rising above the water. Some among us survived the flood. The Master commanded me to gather my people and take them across the waters to the land of the barbarians who lived in caves. There, we would carry out the plan we knew so well.

I gathered my people, and we boarded the Master's great ship. As we rose into the morning sky, the Temple of Light disappeared beneath the rising waters. It vanished from the Earth until the appointed time when it would return. We fled toward the rising sun, and beneath us lay the land of the children of Khem. When we arrived, the barbarians came at us with spears and clubs, filled with rage and intent on destroying the Sons of Atlantis.

I raised my staff and directed a ray of vibration at them, freezing them in place like stones from the mountain. Then I spoke to them calmly, telling them of the greatness of Atlantis and explaining that we were messengers of the Sun. I used my knowledge of magic and science to subdue them until they bowed before me. When I released them, they groveled at my feet in fear.

We lived in the land of Khem for many long years. Following the Master's command, I eventually sent the Sons of Atlantis to distant lands, so that the wisdom of Atlantis could rise again in the future. Through the womb of time, knowledge would once more be reborn in those who seek it.

For a long time, I lived in the land of Khem, using my knowledge to perform great works. The people of Khem grew in understanding, nourished by the wisdom I shared. To retain my power, I opened a path to Amenti, allowing me to live through the ages as a Sun of Atlantis, preserving knowledge and records. The people of Khem became strong, conquering those around them and slowly rising in spiritual strength.

Now I must leave them and descend into the dark halls of Amenti, deep within the Earth, where I will stand once more before the Dweller. Above the entrance to Amenti, I raised a gateway—only a few have the courage to cross it. Over the portal, I built a mighty pyramid, harnessing the power that defies Earth's gravity. Inside, I placed a force-chamber, creating a circular passage that reaches near the top. At the summit, I set a crystal to send a ray through time and space, drawing energy from the ether and focusing it toward the gateway of Amenti.

I built other chambers that seem empty but hide the keys to Amenti within them. Only those who dare to explore the dark realms may enter, but first, they must purify themselves through fasting. Those who seek the mysteries must lie in the stone sarcophagus within my chamber, and then the hidden truths will be revealed. Even in the depths of the Earth, I will meet them. I, Thoth, the Lord of Wisdom, will dwell with them always.

I built the Great Pyramid, designing it to align with the forces of the Earth, so it would burn with energy for eternity and stand through the ages. Inside, I placed my knowledge of magic and science, ensuring I could return from Amenti. While my body sleeps in the halls, my soul will roam freely, incarnating among humans in different forms, including as Hermes, thrice-born.

I serve as the Dweller's messenger on Earth, following his commands to guide many toward enlightenment. Now I return to the halls of Amenti, leaving behind fragments of my wisdom. Keep the Dweller's command: Always lift your gaze toward the light. In time, you will become one with the Master, united with the All. I leave now, but remember my teachings. Live by them, and I will be with you, guiding you into the light. As the portal opens before me, I descend into the night's darkness.

Deep in the heart of the Earth lie the Halls of Amenti, beneath the sunken islands of Atlantis. These halls are places for both the living and the dead, illuminated by the fire of the infinite All. In a distant past, the Children of Light observed humanity's struggle, seeing that people were bound by forces beyond them. They knew that only by breaking free could humans rise from Earth toward the Sun. The Children of Light took human form and came down to Earth, saying, "We are beings formed from the dust of space, part of the infinite All. Though we live as humans, we are not entirely like them."

They created vast spaces beneath the Earth's surface, far from where humans lived, surrounding these halls with powerful forces to protect them from harm. They built other spaces nearby, filling them with life and light from above. In these hidden places, they built the Halls of Amenti to dwell there eternally, living with endless life.

Thirty-two of the Children of Light came among humans, seeking to free them from the darkness and the forces that bound them. In the Halls of Life, a bright, flaming flower grew, expanding and driving away the darkness. At its center, they placed a powerful ray, filling all who came near with life and light. Around the flower, they arranged thirty-two thrones, where the Children of Light sat, bathed in its radiance and filled with the eternal light.

Over the ages, they placed their original bodies in these halls, reawakening them every thousand years with the life-giving light, which quickened their spirits. Though they appeared to sleep, their souls moved freely through the bodies of men, guiding and teaching them. As their bodies rested, they incarnated among humans, leading them from darkness into the light. In the Halls of Life, they kept knowledge unknown to humanity, living forever beneath the cool fire of life.

At times, they awakened from their rest, coming forth as lights among people, infinite beings among finite men. Those who rise from darkness into light are freed from the Halls of Amenti and the Flower of Life.

With wisdom as their guide, they pass from among men to join the Masters of Life, free from the bonds of darkness. In the center of the radiant flower sit seven Lords from realms beyond time, guiding humanity with infinite wisdom along the path through time. Though they are silent and hidden, their power is immense, and their knowledge is endless.

Drawing from the Life force, different yet connected to the children of men. Though different, they are also One with the Children of Light. They guard and watch over the forces that bind humanity, ready to release them when the time for enlightenment arrives.

At the forefront sits the Veiled Presence, the Lord of Lords, the infinite Nine, standing above the Lords of the Cycles—Three, Four, Five, Six, Seven, and Eight—each with a purpose and unique power, guiding and shaping human destiny. They sit in strength and wisdom, untouched by time or space. Though not of this world, they are connected to it, like Elder Brothers to humanity. With wisdom, they judge and observe, watching how the Light grows within mankind.

The Dweller led me before them, and I witnessed him blend with the ONE from above. A voice came forth, saying, "Thoth, you are great among the children of men. From this moment, you are free from the Halls of Amenti, a Master of Life among men. Death will come to you only if you desire it. Drink from the well of Life for all eternity, for Life is now yours to take. Death is yours to command at will. Stay here or leave when you wish; Amenti is open to you, a Sun among men. Take Life in any form you choose, Child of the Light who has grown among humanity.

Though free, you must always labor along the path of Light. You have taken one step on the endless journey upward, but the mountain of Light stretches infinitely before you. Every step you take raises the mountain higher; each bit of progress makes the goal seem farther away. You will forever move toward infinite Wisdom, but the goal will always stay just out of reach. You are now free from the Halls of Amenti."

Thank you for Reading

You've Just Read a Piece of the Greatest Library Ever Rebuilt

Thank you for reading.

This book is one of thousands we're restoring, reimagining, and translating as part of the **Modern Library of Alexandria** — a global movement to preserve and share humanity's most important ideas.

What was once lost to fire and time is now rising again — not just as memory, but as living, breathing knowledge, freely accessible to all.

What You Can Do Next:

- **Keep Reading.**

  Discover more legendary works — in beautiful print, audiobook, or digital form — at LibraryofAlexandria.com.

- **Build Your Own Library.**

  Every title is available as a paperback, hardcover, or collectible boxset — at true printing cost. Craft a personal library worthy of display.

- **Spread the Light.**

  Share this book. Tell others about the movement. Help us translate every timeless work into every language, so no reader is ever left behind.

By finishing this book, you've already taken part in something extraordinary.

Join us at LibraryofAlexandria.com

Together, we're rebuilding the greatest library the world has ever known.

With appreciation,
The Modern Library of Alexandria Team

Visit:

www.libraryofalexandria.com

Or scan the code below:

www.ingramcontent.com/pod-product-compliance
Lightning Source LLC
Chambersburg PA
CBHW010733270326
41934CB00016B/3466